Basics

Casting on (CO)
1 Pull the yarn end from the center of the skein and make a loop, leaving a 6-in. (15cm) tail.
2 Insert the needle into the loop as shown. Tighten the loop around your needle. This counts as your first stitch.
3 Hold the needle with the first stitch in your left hand, keeping the tail in front of the needle and the yarn from the skein in back of the needle.
4 Hold the empty needle in your right hand and slide its tip through the stitch on the left needle from left to right (from the front of the stitch to the back). The needles will form an X, with the right needle behind the left needle.
5 Hold the crossed needles between your left thumb and forefinger. Using your right hand, wrap the yarn from the skein counterclockwise around the tip of the right needle. Pull the tip of the right needle down and through the stitch, pulling the new loop through.
6 Gently stretch the loop on the right needle.
7 Working from left to right, slide the tip of the left needle through the loop on the right needle as shown.
8 Slide the right needle out of the loop, leaving

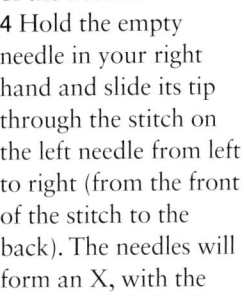

two loops on the left needle. Pull gently to tighten the second stitch. Slide the tip of the right needle into the second stitch and repeat steps 4–7 until you have cast on the required number of stitches.

Making a knit stitch (k)
1 Hold the needle with the cast-on stitches in your left hand, with the first stitch (the last cast-on stitch) about 1 in. (2.5cm) from the needle tip. Slide the tip of the right needle into the first stitch, forming an X with the needles. Wrap the yarn from the skein around the tip of the right needle as shown.
2 Slide the right needle and its loop down through the middle of the stitch, as in step 5 of casting on.
3 Slide the stitch off the left needle, creating a loop on the right needle. Repeat steps 1–2 until all of the stitches have been knit off the left needle; this completes your first row. Switch the empty needle to your right hand and the full one to your left hand.

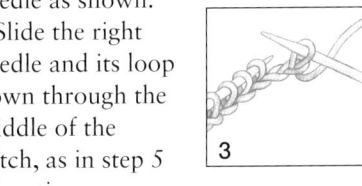

Making a purl stitch (p)
1 With the yarn in front of the left needle, slide the tip of the right needle from right to left through the first stitch. The needles will form an X, with the right needle in front.
2 Wrap the yarn counterclockwise around the tip of the right needle.

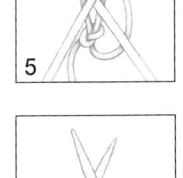

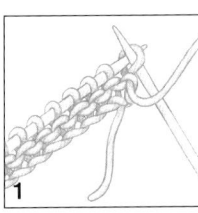

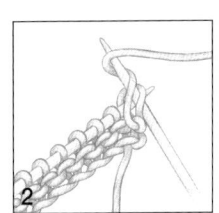

3 Slide the right needle from front to back through the center of the stitch.
4 Pull the loop off the left needle, creating a loop on the right needle. Repeat until the row is complete.

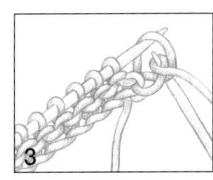

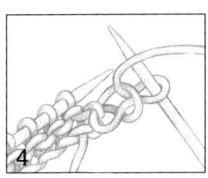

Slipping a stitch (sl)
A slipped stitch is moved from one needle to the other without being knit or purled. To slip a stitch on a knit row, insert the tip of the right needle as if to knit. Slide the stitch off the left needle and onto the right. To slip a stitch on a purl row, insert the tip of the right needle as if to purl. Slide the stitch off the left needle and onto the right.

Increasing (inc)
Increasing means adding more stitches to a row. To make a simple increase, knit into the front and back of an existing stitch. You can do the same with purl stitches.
1 To add a knit stitch, slide the right needle into the stitch, wrap the yarn around the right

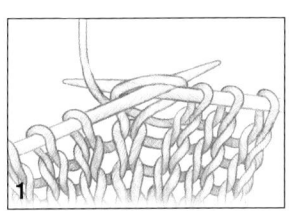

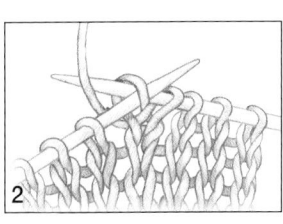

needle, and pull the loop down through the middle of the stitch. Do not drop the stitch off the left needle.
2 Bring the right needle to the back of the loop and knit into it, dropping the loop off the needle when finished.

Decreasing (dec)
Decreasing is reducing the number of

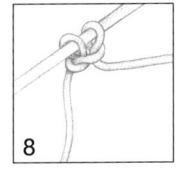

Basics

stitches in a row. Depending on the pattern, the decreased stitches may need to slant to the left or right.

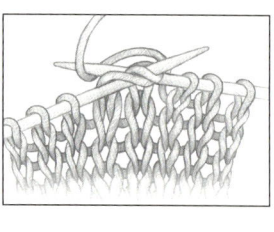

To make a right-slanting decrease on a knit row, work until you reach the stitches to be decreased. Insert the right needle from left to right through both stitches as shown, and knit the stitches together. This is abbreviated as "k2tog."

To make a right-slanting decrease on a purl row, insert the right needle from right to left through both stitches. Purl the stitches.

To make a left-slanting decrease, slip a stitch and knit or purl the next stitch normally. Then slide the tip of the left needle under the slipped stitch, pull it up and over the knit or purled stitch, and drop it off the needle.

Yarn over (yo)
Before knitting a stitch, bring the yarn to the front and over the top of the right needle (this leaves an extra loop on the needle). Knit the next stitch.

Binding off (BO)
Place the full needle in your left hand and the empty needle in your right. Knit two stitches onto the right needle.
1 Slide the tip of the left needle into the outer stitch, pull it up and over the inner stitch, and drop it off the needle.

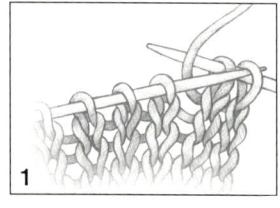

2 This leaves one loop on the right needle. To continue, knit another stitch onto the right needle and repeat step 1.
3 When you reach the last stitch on the left needle, knit it onto the right needle and repeat step 1. One loop remains on the needle. Cut the yarn, remove the loop, pass the yarn through the loop, and tighten.

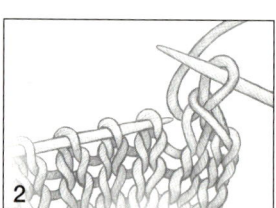

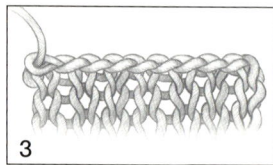

Picking up stitches
To pick up stitches from the side of a piece, slide your right needle between the bars along the side of the edge, wrap the yarn around the needle, and pull it

through. Continue, spacing stitches evenly, until you have picked up the required amount of stitches.

Weaving in ends
Once all stitches have been bound off, the yarn ends need to be woven in. Thread the remaining yarn through a yarn needle and weave it in and out of stitches on the wrong side of the fabric. Trim the excess yarn when finished.

Felting
When 100% wool yarn is wetted and agitated, the fibers and are bound together permanently. This creates a sturdy fabric that's excellent for purses, bags, and totes.

To felt an item, place it in the washing machine on a hot wash cycle. If you wish, add some clothing—blue jeans work well—to the cycle, to assist in agitating the item. Check the item frequently, to avoid overshrinking, and remove it before the rinse cycle begins.

Lark's head knot
1 Fold a cord in half and lay it behind a length of yarn with the fold pointing up.
2 Bring the fold around the strand from back to front. Pull

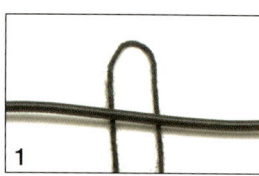

the ends through the fold and tighten.

Overhand knot
Make a loop and pass the working end through it. Pull the ends to tighten the knot.

Whipstitch
Whipstitch is used to hand-sew seams. Bring the needle through the material on

the bottom side of the opening and push it through the material on the upper side of the opening at an angle. Repeat until the opening has been closed.

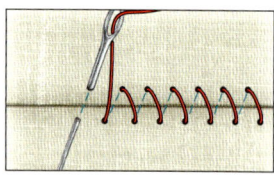

OTHER ABBREVIATIONS

Double-pointed needles: dpns
Pass slipped stitch over: PSSO
Right side: RS
Slip, slip, knit: SSK
Stitch/stitches: st/sts
Stockinette stitch (alternating between knit and purl rows): St st
Wrong side: WS

Sophisticated chenille handbag

Soft chenille yarn creates a tweed appearance for this sturdy handbag.

Before beginning, make a test swatch. Work in stockinette stitch with the yarn held double; a 5-in. (12.cm) swatch should contain 12 stitches.

bag

[1] With size 11 (8mm) needles and the yarn held double, CO 12 stitches.
[2] Work 3 in. (7.6cm) in St st. End with a WS row.
[3] Begin increase rows, working as follows:
Row 1: (K1, inc 1) across – 18 stitches.
Row 2: P across.
Row 3: (K1, inc1) across – 27 stitches.
[4] Work even in St st until the piece measures 18 in. (46cm). End with a WS row.
[5] Begin decrease rows, working as follows:
Row 1: (K1, k2tog) across – 18 stitches.
Row 2: P across.
Row 3: (K1, k2tog) across – 12 stitches.
[6] Work even in St st for 3 in. Your piece should measure approximately 21 in. (53cm). BO and weave in ends.
[7] Fold the bag in half. Starting at the bottom, seam 6 in. (15cm) of each side.
[8] Fold a 3-in. edge over each handle and sew in place.

I-cord and trim

[1] Using size 8 (5mm) double-pointed needles and a single strand of yarn, CO five stitches.
Row 1: K across. Slide stitches to the other end of the needle.
Row 2: K across, keeping yarn taut across the back of the needle. Repeat rows 1 and 2 until the I-cord measures 5 in. (12.7cm). BO and weave in ends.
[2] Repeat to make another 5-in. I-cord.
[3] Sew an I-cord to each side of the bag, just below the handles.
[4] Make a yarn tassel and attach it to the right-hand side of the front I-cord. ○
– *Monette Satterfield*

MATERIALS

- 2 skeins (180 yds./164.5m) medium-weight chenille yarn (Caron Jewel Box, #0005 Tigereye)
- straight knitting needles, size 11 (8mm)
- double-pointed needles, size 8 (5mm)
- black plastic purse handles (Darice Craft Designer, #1972-162)

Mini tote with fur trim

Use a colorful, textured yarn for this simple, fur-trimmed tote.

Before starting the pattern, make swatches to check your gauge. For the bag body, work in stockinette stitch; 12 stitches should measure 3½ in. (8.8cm). For the trim, work in garter stitch (knit every row) with the yarn held double; seven stitches should measure 2 in. (5cm). Switch needle sizes if needed.

Support the bag bottom with a piece of heavy cardboard. Cut a piece to 2½ x 8½ in. (6.3 x 22cm). When the bag is finished, trim the cardboard to fit and place it in the bag bottom.

bag
[1] Using size 10½ (6.5mm) needles and the heavy worsted yarn, CO 30 stitches.
[2] Work 1 in. (2.5cm) in St st. End with a WS row.
[3] Purl the next RS row to create a turning ridge.
[4] Continue working in St st until the piece measures 7 in. (17.8cm). End with a WS row.
[5] Begin decreases: At the beginning and end of the next four rows, k2tog (22 stitches remain on the needle after the four decrease rows).
[6] Work two rows even. Center the bottom of the bag.
[7] Begin increases: At the beginning and end of the next four rows, inc1 (30 stitches remain on the needle after the increase rows).
[8] Work even in St st until the piece measures 14 in. (35.5cm) or matches the first side from the center bottom.
[9] Work a purl turning ridge as in step 3.
[10] Work 1 in. more in St st.
[11] BO and weave in ends.
[12] Fold the bag in half and seam the sides. Fold 1 in. of the top edge over to the inside of the bag at each turning ridge, and stitch to secure.

I-cord handles
[1] CO 4 stitches with size 8 (5mm) double-pointed needles and heavy worsted yarn.
Row 1: K. Slide stitches to the other end of the needle.
Row 2: K, making sure to keep the yarn taut across the back of the stitches.
[2] Repeat rows 1 and 2 until the cord measures 21 in. (53cm). BO and weave in ends.
[3] Repeat steps 1–2 to make another I-cord.
[4] Use your fingers to gently create an opening 2 in. from each end of the bag (photo a). Insert one cord end through an opening from the inside to the outside of the bag, and knot the end (photo b). Repeat with the remaining cord ends.
[5] Stitch the handle securely to the inside of the bag.

fur trim
[1] Using size 10½ (6.5mm) needles and the fur novelty yarn held double, CO seven stitches.
[2] Work in garter stitch until the piece fits around the top of the bag.
[3] BO and weave in ends.
[4] Sew the completed trim to the top of the bag, covering the purl turning ridges.

– Monette Satterfield

MATERIALS
- skein (150 yds./137m) heavy worsted yarn (Sirdar Stampata, Plum Marbles #789)
- skein (75 yds./68.5m) fur novelty yarn (Marks & Kattens Peluche, #275 Fuchsia)
- straight knitting needles, size 10½ (6.5mm) or size needed to obtain gauge
- double-pointed knitting needles, size 8 (5mm)
- heavy cardboard for bag bottom

[a]

[b]

Ribbed wool purse

Create an expandable purse with 2 x 2 ribbing. Add scalloped trim with a crochet hook.

[1] Leaving a 50-in. (1.2m) tail, CO 42 stitches. Make note of the tail's position to use as a reference; on the right side of the work, the tail will always be to the right.
Row 1: P4. (K2, p2) until four stitches are left. P4.
Row 2: K4. (P2, k2) until four stitches are left. K4.
Rows 3–4: Repeat rows 1 and 2. Turn and end with the RS facing.
Row 5: P4. (K2, p2) until you reach the 11th stitch, and then P1, yo knitwise, sl 1 purlwise, K1, PSSO, and K1 to create an open eyelet stitch. Continue in k2, p2 ribbing until you reach the 31st stitch, and create another open eyelet stitch. Work k2, p2 ribbing until four stitches are left. P4.
Rows 6–111: Repeat rows 1 and 2 until piece measures 27 in. (68.5cm).
Row 112: Repeat row 5 to add two more open eyelet stitches, making sure the RS is facing.
Rows 113–116: Repeat rows 2 and 1.
[2] BO, leaving a 45-in. (1.1m) tail.
[3] With the right sides facing, fold the piece in half crosswise, so the ribs are vertical. Starting at the top, seam the sides with an overcast, or whip, stitch (Basics, p. 3). Make sure to catch only the stitches at the very edge, and stop when 4 in. (10cm) away from the folded bottom edge.
[4] Fold the bottom up (**figure 1**) to meet the midpoint of the side seam. Whipstitch the edges together in one direction, then work back over in the opposite direction. Weave in loose ends.
[5] Cut a 45-in. length of yarn and repeat steps 3 and 4 to seam the opposite side.
[6] Use the crochet hook to give the purse a scalloped upper edge (**figure 2**). Begin at the side seams of the right edge. Into the loops of the first stitch, add *1sc, 1hdc, 4dc, 1hdc, 1sc (see p. 9 for crochet stitches and abbreviations). Repeat from * across the front of the bag to the opposite side seam. Note: The second half of the bag's edge is the beginning of the knitting; be sure to catch two stitch loops for each crochet stitch. Repeat from * for the remainder of the bag.
[7] Following the manufacturer's

Crochet stitches

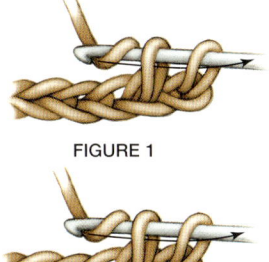

FIGURE 1

FIGURE 2

single crochet (sc)
[1] Insert the hook through the front and back of the first stitch from the hook. Yarn over and draw through the chain (two loops remain on the hook).
[2] Yarn over and draw through both loops (one loop remains on the hook).

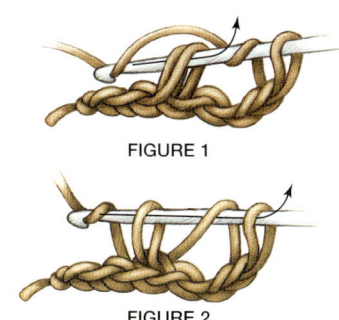

FIGURE 1

FIGURE 2

half double crochet (hdc)
[1] Yarn over. Insert the hook through the first or second stitch from the hook, yarn over, and draw through the stitch (three loops on the hook).
[2] Yarn over and draw through all three loops on the hook (one loop on the hook).

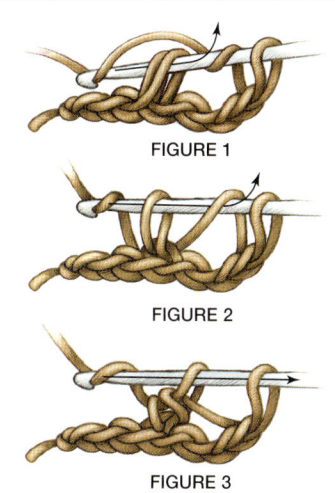

FIGURE 1

FIGURE 2

FIGURE 3

double crochet (dc)
[1] Yarn over. Insert the hook through the second stitch from the hook, yarn over, and draw through the stitch (three loops remain on the hook).
[2] Yarn over and draw through two loops on the hook (two loops remain on the hook).
[3] Yarn over and draw through the remaining two loops on the hook (one loop remains on the hook).

instructions, use the grommet setter to set a grommet into each open eyelet stitch. Be sure to catch the fabric snugly in the grommets before pounding them shut.
[8] Open the brass rings by gently pushing one side away from you and pulling the other side toward you (do not try to unroll the rings). Insert one ring into a left grommet, and carry it through to the right grommet, taking care not to snag the fabric. Close the ring. Repeat with the other ring. Seal each ring opening with a small amount of masking or duct tape.
[9] Using two strands of pearl cotton held together, sc around each ring, fitting the crochet stitches snugly together without overlapping them. (Wind each skein of pearl cotton into a ball before beginning, to avoid tangling.) Fasten off and weave in ends. ● – *Paula Gron*

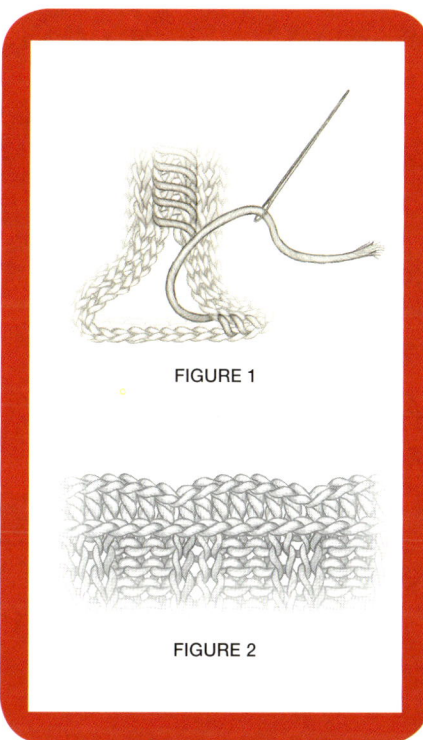

FIGURE 1

FIGURE 2

MATERIALS
- **2** skeins worsted wool yarn (Reynolds Lopi, #308 Blue)
- **4** skeins #3 weight pearl cotton (DMC, #938 Chocolate)
- straight knitting needles, size 10½ (6.5mm)
- crochet hook, size G/6 (4mm)
- ⅜ in. (9mm) brass grommet eyelets
- grommet setter
- **2** 7-in. (18cm) diameter brass rings (Uniek)
- masking or duct tape

"Pumpkin" purse

Knit on circular needles, this round purse provides an opportunity to master decreases.

MATERIALS
- 2 skeins (236 yds.) bulky yarn (Patons Shetland Chunky)
- 16-in. (40.6cm) circular knitting needles, size 7 (4.5mm)
- double-pointed needles, size 7
- steel crochet hook, #9
- tapestry needle, #16
- stitch marker
- 6-in. (15cm) plastic canvas round
- 2 yds. (1.8m) sewing thread to match yarn
- 8 glass lampwork beads with 2mm center holes

Make a test swatch before beginning: CO 17 stitches, and work in the pattern stitch (k2, p2) for 25 rows. The swatch should measure 4 in. (10cm).

bag
[1] Using the circular knitting needles, CO 100 stitches. Place a stitch marker and join, making sure the stitches are not twisted.
Rounds 1 & 2: (K2, p2) 25 times.
Rounds 3 & 4: (P2, k2) 25 times.
Round 5: (K2, p2tog, yo twice) 25 times.
Round 6 (eyelet round): (k2, p1, drop first yo, p the second yo) 25 times.
Rounds 7 & 8: (p2, k2) 25 times.
Rounds 9 & 10: (k2, p2) 25 times.
Round 11: (k9, slp 1, k10) five times.
Round 12: (k8, m1r, k3, m1l, k9) five times – 110 st.
Round 13: (k10, slp 1, k11) 5 times.
Round 14: (k9, m1r, k3, m1l, k10) five times – 120 st.
Round 15: (k11, slp 1) 10 times.
Round 16: K.
[2] Repeat rounds 15–16 until the purse measures 8 in. (20cm) from the beginning. End with a repeat of row 15. Do not cut the yarn.
[3] Begin decreases.
Round 1: (k8, k2tog, k3, skp, k9) five times – 110 st.
Round 2: (k10, slp 1) 10 times.
Round 3: (k7, k2tog, k3, skp, k8) five times – 100 st.
Round 4: (k9, slp 1) 10 times.
Round 5: (k6, k2tog, k3, skp, k7) five times – 90 st.
Round 6: (k8, slp 1) 10 times.
Round 7: (k5, k2tog, k3, skp, k6) five times – 80 st.
Round 8: (k7, slp 1) 10 times.
Round 9: (k4, k2tog, k3, skp, k5) five times – 70 st.
Round 10: (k6, slp 1) 10 times.
Round 11: (k3, k2tog, k3, skp, k4) five times – 60 st.
Round 12: (k5, slp 1) 10 times.
Round 13: (k2, k2tog, k3, skp, k3) five times – 50 st.
Round 14: (k4, slp 1) 10 times.
Round 15: (k1, k2tog, k3, skp, k2) five times – 40 st.
Round 16: (k3, slp 1) 10 times.
Round 17: (k2tog, k3, skp, k1) five times – 30 st.
Round 18: (k2, slp 1) 10 times.
Round 19: (k2tog, k1, skp, k1) five times – 20 st.
Round 20: (k1, slp 1) 10 times.
Round 21: (k2tog, skp) five times – 10 st.
Round 22: k10.
[4] BO, leaving an 18-in. (46cm) tail. Thread the tapestry needle with the yarn. Run the needle through the bound-off edge, pulling the stitches together. Fasten the yarn and weave in ends.
[5] Turn the bag wrong side out. Place the 6-in. (15cm) plastic canvas round in

the center of the bag bottom, and use needle and thread to attach it to the bag. Turn the bag right side out.

twisted cord

[1] Cut 16 yds. (14.6m) of yarn. Fold the piece in half, and attach the ends to a doorknob or other stationary object. Place a pencil in the fold and twist the yarn. Keep twisting until the yarn begins to kink.
[2] Holding the middle of the twisted piece, bring the ends together. Let the middle go so the cord will twist. Tie an overhand knot 8 in. from each end.
[3] Thread the cord through the eyelet holes made on round 5. Tie the ends together with an overhand knot (Basics, p. 3) 1 in. (2.5cm) above the knots in the individual ends.
[4] Open the bag as far as it will go, and pull the excess cord evenly out to the sides. You should have a 13-in. (33cm) loop on each side for the handles. Tie an overhand knot close to the side of the purse on each tie.
[5] Push a #9 steel crochet hook through one of the glass beads. Hook one of the yarn ends of the cord and pull it through the bead. Tie an overhand knot after the bead. Repeat with each cord end. ○
– *Ava Lynne Green*

> **SPECIAL STITCHES**
> **Skp:** Sl a stitch knitwise. Knit the next stitch. PSSO.
> **m1r:** Make a right-slanting increase: Insert the left needle from back to front under the yarn between the last stitch on the right needle and the first stitch on the left. Knit into the front of the new stitch.
> **m1l:** Make a left-slanting increase: Insert the left needle from front to back under the thread between the last stitch on the right needle and the first stitch on the left. Knit into the front of the new stitch.

Yellow "garden" bag

A bright novelty yarn gives the impression of a colorful flower garden at the bottom of this charming felted bag.

MATERIALS
- straight, 16-in. (41cm) circular and double-pointed knitting needles, size 15 (10mm)
- 4 skeins (110 yds./100m) worsted wool yarn (KnitPicks Wool of the Andes, Daffodil)
- skein novelty yarn (Target Funky Fringe)

[a]

[b]

bag
[1] Using the straight needles and the wool held double, CO 15 stitches.
[2] Work 25 rows in garter stitch.
[3] With the circular needles, pick up 20 stitches on each long side, 15 stitches from the short side, and all 15 stitches from the straight needle (**photo a**). You'll have a total of 70 stitches on the circular needle. Place a stitch marker and begin to work in St st. (Because ths project is knit in the round, knit every row to create St st.)
[4] Knit one round with two strands of wool.
[5] Join one strand of novelty yarn, and work in rounds with all three strands for 4 in. (10cm).
[6] Drop the novelty yarn and continue knitting in rounds for another 4 in.
[7] Decrease on the next round: K8, K2tog around.
[8] Purl three rounds.
[9] BO and weave in all ends.

I-cord handle
[1] Using the double-pointed needles, two strands of wool, and one strand of novelty yarn, CO three stitches.
Row 1: K across. Slide stitches to the other end of the needle.
Row 2: K across, keeping yarn taut across the back of the needle. Repeat rows 1 and 2 until the I-cord measures 38 in. (96.5cm). BO and weave in ends.
[2] Starting 3–4 in. (7.6–10cm) from the bag's corners, weave the I-cord in and out. Repeat on the other side, and join the ends. The pre-felted bag should resemble **photo b**.

NEEDLE SUBSTITUTION
If you are unable to find size 15 double-pointed knitting needles locally, you can try ordering them on the Internet. Or you can use the size 15 circular needles; just take extra care to keep the yarn taut and the stitches untwisted as you slide them across the cord.

felting
Felt the bag (Basics) and re-shape while it is still wet. If you wish, fill the bag with plastic wrap or plastic bags to help it hold its shape while drying.
– Sally Kulmaczewski

Roomy felted tote

Feathery novelty yarn accents a brilliant blue tote bag.

[1] With the straight knitting needles and the wool yarn held double, CO 40 stitches. Work 15 rows in garter stitch.
[2] With the circular needle, pick up eight stitches on each short side, 40 stitches from the long side, and all 40 stitches from the needle. You'll have a total of 96 stitches on the circular needle. Place a stitch marker and join to work in St st rounds.
[3] Work 16 rounds in the wool yarn.
[4] Join a strand of the novelty yarn and work six rounds with all three strands.
[5] Drop the novelty yarn and work another 6 in. (15cm) in the wool yarn.
[6] Put eight stitches from each short edge on stitch holders. Switch one of the 40-stitch sides to the straight needles. Using two strands of wool and one strand of novelty yarn, work as follows:
Row 1: K2, K2tog across.
Rows 2 and 3: K.
Row 4: P.
BO. Switch the remaining 40-stitch side to the straight needles, and work in the same manner. BO.
[7] To make the strap, transfer one eight-stitch side to the straight needles. Using two strands of wool, work in the following pattern:
Row 1: Slip a stitch knitwise, K7.
Row 2: Slip a stitch purlwise, P7.
Alternate rows 1 and 2 for 30 in. (76cm). If you want a longer strap, keep repeating rows 1 and 2 until you reach the desired length.
[8] Join the strap to the eight stitches on the remaining stitch holder using a three-needle bind off (see below). If you wish, you can simply sew the stitches together with a tapestry needle. Weave in loose ends.
[9] Felt the bag as described in Basics. Be sure to re-shape the bag while it is still wet. ○ – Sally Kulmaczewski

MATERIALS
- 3 skeins worsted-weight wool yarn (Cascade 220, #8891 Turquoise)
- skein novelty yarn (Bernat Boa, #81205 Peacock)
- straight, 24-in. (61cm) circular, and double-pointed knitting needles, size 15 (10mm)
- stitch marker
- 2 stitch holders

EDITOR'S NOTE
Cascade 220, the yarn used to make this bag, comes in two varieties: wool and superwash (machine-washable). If you choose to work with Cascade, be sure to buy the plain wool; the superwash is not suitable for felting.

Three-Needle Bind-Off
[1] With the right sides facing, hold the two knitting needles in your left hand with the points to the right. Insert a third needle knitwise through the first stitch on the front needle, and then knitwise through the first stitch on the back needle (**photo a**).
[2] Knit the two stitches together, creating one stitch on the third needle (**photo b**).
[3] Repeat with the second stitches on the front and back needles, making a second stitch on the third needle (**photo c**).
[4] Pull the stitch made in step 2 over the stitch made in step 3, leaving one stitch on the needle (**photo d**) as in the standard bind-off.
[5] Repeat steps 2–4 until all of the stitches have been bound off (**photo e**).

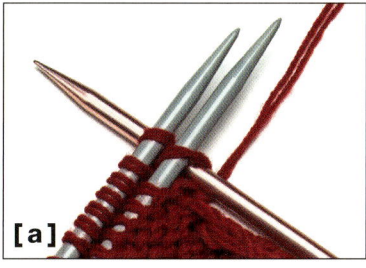
[a]

[b]

[c]

[d]

[e]

Sunset felted tote

Smooth color gradations add drama to this striking felted tote.

Knit the front side of this tote flat until you reach the bottom, and then shape the bottom with short rows on both edges. The back side of the purse is also knit flat, but attached to each side of the front at each row, conveniently seaming the sides as you work. The short rows and seaming will make the purse resemble the toe of a giant sock.

After the front and back are completed and seamed, the purse is turned so the side seams are together in the middle. Each shoulder strap is made by picking up stitches around each seam; the straps are knit flat, shaped by decreases, and joined in the center. An easy triangle pattern enhances the lower portion of each strap.

There is no gauge for this project. Pre-felted, my tote measured approximately 14 x 13¼ in. (35.5 x 33.6cm). After the felting process, it measured 11 x 8½ in. (28 x 22cm). The yarn I used shrank about 37% vertically and 23% horizontally during felting. If you use a different yarn or would like a larger or smaller tote, knit a 4-in. (10cm) square swatch, felt it, and adjust the number of cast-on stitches and rows accordingly.

tote
[1] Using color A yarn, CO 30 stitches.
Rows 1-12: Work in St st.
Rows 13-16: Add a strand of color B yarn, and continue in St st, alternating between color A and color B every stitch and every row. This will make a checkerboard pattern (see **photo a** for an example of the pattern).
Rows 17-29: Work in St st with color B.
Rows 30-33: Add a strand of color C yarn and continue in St st, alternating between color B and color C every stitch and every row.
Rows 34-48: Work in St st with color C.
Rows 49-52: Add a strand of color D yarn and continue in St st, alternating between color C and color D every stitch and every row.
Rows 53-59: Work in St st with color D.
[2] Begin short row shaping to make the rounded end at the bottom of the purse. Work as follows:
Row 1: Work in St st until the last stitch. Turn the fabric.
Row 2: Sl one stitch (there are now two stitches on the working needle) and work in St st until the last stitch at the other end. Turn the fabric.
Row 3: Sl a stitch (there are now two non-worked stitches at this end) and work in St st until there are three stitches left. Turn the fabric.
Row 4: Sl a stitch and work in St st until there are four stitches left. Turn the fabric.
Row 5: Sl a stitch and work in St st until there are five stitches left. Turn the fabric.
Row 6: Sl a stitch and work in St st until there are six stitches left. Turn the fabric.
Row 7: Sl a stitch and work in St st until the fifth stitch (two less than before), beginning to incorporate the non-worked stitches back into the pattern. Turn the fabric.
Row 8: Sl a stitch and work in St st until the fifth stitch (two less than before). Turn the fabric.

Continue in this manner (working down to two less stitches than before) until all of the non-worked stitches are working again. This ends the short-row shaping (see **photo b** for a close-up of the short rows).
[3] Work the back of the purse as you worked the front of the purse, with the colors reversed. You'll also add a step to each row: Attach each new row to the front fabric to make a seam. Looking at the purl side of the front piece, you will notice there are long loops and small knots at the edge of each row (**photo c**). Hook the long loop with the crochet hook and knit or purl it together with the last stitch of each row, creating a seam as you knit (**photos d–e**). Note: The knit rows can be awkward to complete. It is easier to pick up the long loop while working on the purl side (**photo f**); be sure to slip the long loop onto the needle without working a stitch into it so you don't end up accidentally increasing.
[4] Work in St st, seaming as you work, until the back side of the purse is even with the front side. BO all stitches and weave in loose ends.

straps
[1] Mark the center four stitches on both the front and the back of the piece. Arrange the fabric so the marks are at the sides. Using color A, pick up 26 stitches between one set of marks to begin the first shoulder strap.
Row 1: K in color A, adding one color F stitch in the middle.
Row 2: K in color A, adding three color F stitches in the middle.

Chain stitch
[1] Make a loop in the thread, crossing the ball end over the tail. Put the hook through the loop, yarn over the hook, and draw it through the first loop.

[2] Yarn over the hook and draw through the loop. Repeat for the desired number of chain stitches.

MATERIALS
- 6 skeins worsted weight wool yarn (Highland Wool)
  color A (Alpine Violet 1750)
  color B (Boysenberry 1898)
  color C (Candy Cane 2080)
  color D (Burnt Orange 9110)
  color E (Calypso Green 1430)
  color F (Russet 3729)
- straight or circular knitting needles, size 10 (6mm)
- crochet hook, size 7 (4.5mm)
- yarn needle
- large stone donut for closure
- 12 in. (30cm) 24-gauge silver wire
- roundnose pliers

Row 3: K in color A, adding five color F stitches in the middle.

Continue working in this manner, adding two color F stitches to each row to create an inverted triangle. At the same time, you'll be decreasing stitches on each side of alternate rows, so eventually color A will run out of the pattern.

[2] Add in color E, repeating the checkerboard pattern from step 1 of "tote" for four rows with colors E and F.

[3] Drop color F, work several rows with color E, and then begin decreasing until 10 stitches remain on the needle. Work in St st with color E until the strap is the desired length. Do not bind off; place the stitches on a stitch holder or a spare knitting needle.

[4] Repeat steps 1–3 to make the other half of the strap.

[5] Join the two halves using a three-needle bind-off (see p. 15), making sure the straps are not twisted. Since the straps were worked in St st, the edges may curl inward slightly. For a flat, smooth finish, fold the strap in half lengthwise and seam the edges. Weave in all ends.

[6] Turn the bag so the straps are on the sides; you'll notice that the front and back form a slight V. I used color E to add edging here. Use a size 7 (4.5mm) crochet hook to single crochet (p. 9) along the V shape—begin at one end of each checkerboard segment, and work your way across to the other.

See **photos g–h** for close-ups of the straps and the pre-felted tote.

felting & assembly

[1] Felt the piece as described in Basics (I added a few drops of dish detergent to assist the process). Remove the tote before the rinse cycle begins, and shape while still wet. Let dry thoroughly.

[2] Use roundnose pliers and your fingers to loop and twist 12 in. (30cm) of 24-gauge wire over a large stone donut. Sew the embellished donut to the front of the purse.

[3] Using a chain stitch (p. 17), crochet a cord long enough to fit over the closure. When the chain is the desired length, turn and chain stitch along the entire length to create a thicker cord.

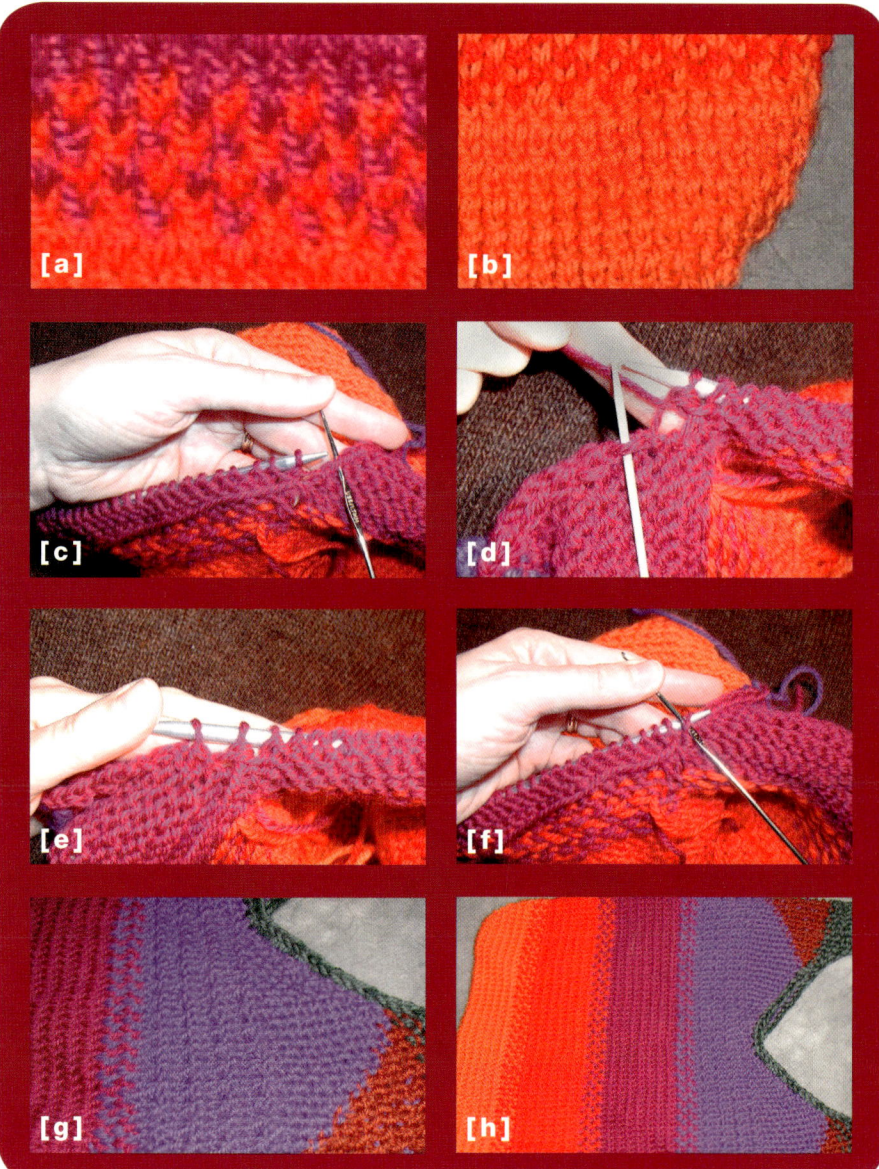

Fasten off and sew the double chain to the inside back of the purse.

–Susan Forbes

AUTHOR'S NOTE:
In **photos g** and **h** above, you'll note that the first 12 rows (from step 1 of "tote") look textured. For felting interest, I used a geometric pattern stitch here. If you'd like to do the same, replace step 1 with this pattern:
Row 1: K across.
Row 2: P across.
Row 3: K2tog across.
Row 4: (P1, inc1) across.
Repeat twice.